50 Easy and Elegant Cupcake Recipes

By: Kelly Johnson

Table of Contents

- Classic Vanilla Cupcakes
- Chocolate Fudge Cupcakes
- Red Velvet Cupcakes
- Lemon Meringue Cupcakes
- Strawberry Shortcake Cupcakes
- Salted Caramel Cupcakes
- Mocha Cupcakes
- Raspberry Chocolate Cupcakes
- Peanut Butter Cup Cupcakes
- Almond Joy Cupcakes
- Coconut Cream Cupcakes
- S'mores Cupcakes
- Funfetti Cupcakes
- Pumpkin Spice Cupcakes
- Matcha Green Tea Cupcakes
- Blueberry Cheesecake Cupcakes
- Churro Cupcakes
- Lemon Poppy Seed Cupcakes
- Nutella-Filled Cupcakes
- Carrot Cake Cupcakes
- Chocolate Mint Cupcakes
- Cherry Almond Cupcakes
- Tiramisu Cupcakes
- Lavender Honey Cupcakes
- Key Lime Pie Cupcakes
- Chocolate Hazelnut Cupcakes
- Coconut Pineapple Cupcakes
- Champagne Cupcakes
- Cookies and Cream Cupcakes
- Pineapple Upside-Down Cupcakes
- White Chocolate Raspberry Cupcakes
- Maple Bacon Cupcakes
- Cinnamon Roll Cupcakes
- Hot Cocoa Cupcakes
- White Chocolate Macadamia Cupcakes

- Mocha Hazelnut Cupcakes
- Mint Chocolate Chip Cupcakes
- Peanut Butter Banana Cupcakes
- Oreo Cupcakes
- Apple Cinnamon Cupcakes
- Chocolate Cherry Cupcakes
- Pecan Praline Cupcakes
- Funfetti Birthday Cupcakes
- Chocolate Raspberry Ganache Cupcakes
- Blackberry Lemon Cupcakes
- Red Wine Chocolate Cupcakes
- Butter Pecan Cupcakes
- Dark Chocolate Espresso Cupcakes
- Maple Pecan Cupcakes
- Gingerbread Cupcakes

Classic Vanilla Cupcakes

Ingredients:

- 1 ½ cups all-purpose flour
- 1 ½ tsp baking powder
- ½ tsp salt
- ½ cup unsalted butter, softened
- 1 cup granulated sugar
- 2 large eggs
- 1 tsp vanilla extract
- ½ cup milk

Instructions:

1. Preheat oven to 350°F (175°C) and line a muffin tin with paper liners.
2. In a bowl, whisk flour, baking powder, and salt.
3. In another bowl, cream butter and sugar until light and fluffy.
4. Add eggs one at a time, beating well after each addition.
5. Mix in vanilla extract.
6. Gradually add dry ingredients, alternating with milk, until just combined.
7. Divide batter evenly into cupcake liners.
8. Bake for 18-20 minutes, or until a toothpick inserted comes out clean.
9. Cool and frost with your favorite icing.

Chocolate Fudge Cupcakes

Ingredients:

- 1 ½ cups all-purpose flour
- 1 ¼ cups granulated sugar
- ¾ cup unsweetened cocoa powder
- 1 tsp baking powder
- 1 tsp baking soda
- ½ tsp salt
- 2 large eggs
- 1 cup milk
- ½ cup vegetable oil
- 1 tsp vanilla extract
- 1 cup boiling water

Instructions:

1. Preheat oven to 350°F (175°C) and line a muffin tin with paper liners.
2. In a large bowl, mix flour, sugar, cocoa powder, baking powder, baking soda, and salt.
3. Add eggs, milk, oil, and vanilla, and mix until smooth.
4. Gradually add boiling water, mixing until smooth and thin.
5. Pour the batter into the muffin tin.
6. Bake for 18-20 minutes, or until a toothpick inserted comes out clean.
7. Cool and frost with chocolate frosting.

Red Velvet Cupcakes

Ingredients:

- 1 ½ cups all-purpose flour
- 1 cup granulated sugar
- 1 tsp baking soda
- ½ tsp salt
- 1 tbsp cocoa powder
- 1 large egg
- 1 cup buttermilk
- ½ cup vegetable oil
- 1 tsp vanilla extract
- 1 oz red food coloring

Instructions:

1. Preheat oven to 350°F (175°C) and line a muffin tin with paper liners.
2. In a bowl, whisk flour, sugar, baking soda, salt, and cocoa powder.
3. In another bowl, beat together egg, buttermilk, oil, vanilla, and food coloring.
4. Gradually add dry ingredients to wet ingredients, mixing until smooth.
5. Divide the batter evenly among cupcake liners.
6. Bake for 18-20 minutes, or until a toothpick inserted comes out clean.
7. Cool and frost with cream cheese frosting.

Lemon Meringue Cupcakes

Ingredients:

- 1 ½ cups all-purpose flour
- 1 tsp baking powder
- ½ tsp salt
- ½ cup unsalted butter, softened
- 1 cup granulated sugar
- 2 large eggs
- 1 tsp vanilla extract
- 1/3 cup lemon juice
- 2 tbsp lemon zest
- ¼ cup milk
- 3 large egg whites
- ½ cup granulated sugar (for meringue)

Instructions:

1. Preheat oven to 350°F (175°C) and line a muffin tin with paper liners.
2. In a bowl, whisk flour, baking powder, and salt.
3. In another bowl, cream butter and sugar until fluffy, then add eggs and vanilla.
4. Mix in lemon juice, lemon zest, and milk. Gradually add the dry ingredients.
5. Divide the batter evenly among cupcake liners.
6. Bake for 18-20 minutes, or until a toothpick inserted comes out clean.
7. For the meringue, beat egg whites until soft peaks form, then add sugar and beat until stiff peaks form.
8. Spoon meringue over cooled cupcakes and bake for an additional 5-7 minutes at 350°F until golden.

Strawberry Shortcake Cupcakes

Ingredients:

- 1 ½ cups all-purpose flour
- 1 tsp baking powder
- ¼ tsp salt
- ½ cup unsalted butter, softened
- 1 cup granulated sugar
- 2 large eggs
- 1 tsp vanilla extract
- 1/3 cup milk
- 1 cup fresh strawberries, chopped
- Whipped cream for topping

Instructions:

1. Preheat oven to 350°F (175°C) and line a muffin tin with paper liners.
2. In a bowl, mix flour, baking powder, and salt.
3. In another bowl, cream butter and sugar until fluffy, then add eggs and vanilla.
4. Gradually mix in the dry ingredients, followed by milk.
5. Fold in chopped strawberries.
6. Divide the batter evenly among cupcake liners.
7. Bake for 18-20 minutes, or until a toothpick inserted comes out clean.
8. Cool and top with whipped cream and more strawberries.

Salted Caramel Cupcakes

Ingredients:

- 1 ½ cups all-purpose flour
- 1 tsp baking powder
- ½ tsp salt
- ½ cup unsalted butter, softened
- 1 cup brown sugar
- 2 large eggs
- 1 tsp vanilla extract
- 1/2 cup milk
- ½ cup caramel sauce
- Sea salt for garnish

Instructions:

1. Preheat oven to 350°F (175°C) and line a muffin tin with paper liners.
2. In a bowl, whisk flour, baking powder, and salt.
3. In another bowl, cream butter and brown sugar until fluffy, then add eggs and vanilla.
4. Gradually add the dry ingredients and milk, mixing until smooth.
5. Divide batter evenly among cupcake liners and bake for 18-20 minutes.
6. Once cooled, drizzle with caramel sauce and sprinkle with sea salt.

Mocha Cupcakes

Ingredients:

- 1 ½ cups all-purpose flour
- 1 cup granulated sugar
- ½ cup unsweetened cocoa powder
- 1 tsp baking powder
- ½ tsp baking soda
- ¼ tsp salt
- 1 cup brewed coffee, cooled
- 1 egg
- ½ cup vegetable oil
- 1 tsp vanilla extract

Instructions:

1. Preheat oven to 350°F (175°C) and line a muffin tin with paper liners.
2. In a bowl, mix flour, sugar, cocoa powder, baking powder, baking soda, and salt.
3. In another bowl, whisk together brewed coffee, egg, oil, and vanilla.
4. Combine the wet and dry ingredients until smooth.
5. Divide the batter evenly and bake for 18-20 minutes.
6. Cool and frost with chocolate or coffee-flavored frosting.

Raspberry Chocolate Cupcakes

Ingredients:

- 1 ½ cups all-purpose flour
- 1 cup granulated sugar
- 1 tsp baking powder
- ½ cup unsweetened cocoa powder
- 1 egg
- ½ cup milk
- ½ cup vegetable oil
- 1 tsp vanilla extract
- ½ cup fresh raspberries

Instructions:

1. Preheat oven to 350°F (175°C) and line a muffin tin with paper liners.
2. In a bowl, mix flour, sugar, baking powder, and cocoa powder.
3. In another bowl, whisk together egg, milk, oil, and vanilla.
4. Gradually add wet ingredients to dry ingredients, mixing until smooth.
5. Gently fold in raspberries.
6. Divide batter evenly among cupcake liners and bake for 18-20 minutes.
7. Cool and frost with chocolate ganache or raspberry buttercream.

Peanut Butter Cup Cupcakes

Ingredients:

- 1 ½ cups all-purpose flour
- 1 tsp baking powder
- ½ tsp baking soda
- ¼ tsp salt
- 1 cup peanut butter
- 1 cup granulated sugar
- 2 large eggs
- 1 tsp vanilla extract
- 1 cup milk
- ¼ cup chocolate chips (optional)

Instructions:

1. Preheat oven to 350°F (175°C) and line a muffin tin with paper liners.
2. In a bowl, mix flour, baking powder, baking soda, and salt.
3. In another bowl, beat peanut butter and sugar until smooth, then add eggs and vanilla.
4. Gradually add dry ingredients to the wet ingredients and mix in milk.
5. Fold in chocolate chips if using.
6. Bake for 18-20 minutes, or until a toothpick comes out clean.
7. Cool and frost with peanut butter frosting.

Almond Joy Cupcakes

Ingredients:

- 1 ½ cups all-purpose flour
- 1 tsp baking powder
- 1 tsp cocoa powder
- ½ cup unsweetened coconut flakes
- ½ cup chopped almonds
- 1 cup granulated sugar
- 2 large eggs
- ½ cup milk
- ½ cup vegetable oil
- 1 tsp vanilla extract

Instructions:

1. Preheat oven to 350°F (175°C) and line a muffin tin with paper liners.
2. In a bowl, mix flour, baking powder, cocoa powder, coconut flakes, and chopped almonds.
3. In another bowl, whisk together sugar, eggs, milk, oil, and vanilla.
4. Gradually add the dry ingredients to the wet ingredients until smooth.
5. Bake for 18-20 minutes, or until a toothpick comes out clean.
6. Cool and frost with chocolate frosting, garnishing with coconut and almonds.

Coconut Cream Cupcakes

Ingredients:

- 1 ½ cups all-purpose flour
- 1 tsp baking powder
- ½ tsp baking soda
- ½ tsp salt
- 1 cup coconut cream
- 1 cup granulated sugar
- 2 large eggs
- 1 tsp vanilla extract
- ¼ cup shredded coconut

Instructions:

1. Preheat oven to 350°F (175°C) and line a muffin tin with paper liners.
2. In a bowl, mix flour, baking powder, baking soda, and salt.
3. In another bowl, whisk together coconut cream, sugar, eggs, and vanilla.
4. Gradually add the dry ingredients to the wet ingredients, then fold in shredded coconut.
5. Bake for 18-20 minutes, or until a toothpick comes out clean.
6. Cool and frost with coconut cream frosting.

S'mores Cupcakes

Ingredients:

- 1 ½ cups all-purpose flour
- 1 cup granulated sugar
- 1 tsp baking powder
- ½ tsp baking soda
- ½ cup unsweetened cocoa powder
- 1 egg
- 1 cup milk
- ¼ cup vegetable oil
- 1 tsp vanilla extract
- ½ cup graham cracker crumbs
- ¼ cup mini marshmallows
- ¼ cup chocolate chips

Instructions:

1. Preheat oven to 350°F (175°C) and line a muffin tin with paper liners.
2. In a bowl, mix flour, sugar, baking powder, baking soda, and cocoa powder.
3. In another bowl, whisk together egg, milk, oil, and vanilla.
4. Gradually add the wet ingredients to the dry ingredients and stir until smooth.
5. Fold in graham cracker crumbs, marshmallows, and chocolate chips.
6. Divide batter evenly among cupcake liners and bake for 18-20 minutes.
7. Cool and top with marshmallow fluff or toasted marshmallows and a drizzle of chocolate.

Funfetti Cupcakes

Ingredients:

- 1 ½ cups all-purpose flour
- 1 tbsp sugar
- 1 tsp baking powder
- ½ tsp salt
- 1 cup unsalted butter, softened
- 1 cup granulated sugar
- 2 large eggs
- 1 tsp vanilla extract
- ½ cup sprinkles
- ½ cup milk

Instructions:

1. Preheat oven to 350°F (175°C) and line a muffin tin with paper liners.
2. In a bowl, mix flour, sugar, baking powder, and salt.
3. In another bowl, cream butter and sugar until fluffy, then add eggs and vanilla.
4. Gradually mix in the dry ingredients, alternating with milk.
5. Fold in sprinkles.
6. Divide batter evenly among cupcake liners and bake for 18-20 minutes.
7. Cool and frost with buttercream and more sprinkles.

Pumpkin Spice Cupcakes

Ingredients:

- 1 ½ cups all-purpose flour
- 1 tsp baking powder
- 1 tsp cinnamon
- ½ tsp nutmeg
- ¼ tsp ground ginger
- ½ tsp salt
- 1 cup pumpkin puree
- 2 large eggs
- 1 cup sugar
- ½ cup vegetable oil
- 1 tsp vanilla extract

Instructions:

1. Preheat oven to 350°F (175°C) and line a muffin tin with paper liners.
2. In a bowl, whisk flour, baking powder, cinnamon, nutmeg, ginger, and salt.
3. In another bowl, whisk together pumpkin, eggs, sugar, oil, and vanilla.
4. Gradually add the dry ingredients to the wet ingredients and mix until smooth.
5. Divide batter evenly and bake for 18-20 minutes.
6. Cool and frost with cream cheese frosting or whipped cream.

Matcha Green Tea Cupcakes

Ingredients:

- 1 ½ cups all-purpose flour
- 1 tbsp sugar
- 1 tsp baking powder
- 2 tsp matcha green tea powder
- ½ tsp salt
- 1 cup milk
- 2 eggs
- ½ cup unsalted butter, softened
- 1 tsp vanilla extract

Instructions:

1. Preheat oven to 350°F (175°C) and line a muffin tin with paper liners.
2. In a bowl, mix flour, sugar, baking powder, matcha powder, and salt.
3. In another bowl, whisk together milk, eggs, butter, and vanilla.
4. Gradually combine the wet and dry ingredients and mix until smooth.
5. Divide batter evenly among cupcake liners and bake for 18-20 minutes.
6. Cool and frost with matcha buttercream or whipped cream.

Blueberry Cheesecake Cupcakes

Ingredients:

- 1 ½ cups all-purpose flour
- 1 tsp baking powder
- ½ tsp salt
- 1 cup granulated sugar
- 1 cup cream cheese, softened
- 2 large eggs
- 1 tsp vanilla extract
- ½ cup fresh blueberries

Instructions:

1. Preheat oven to 350°F (175°C) and line a muffin tin with paper liners.
2. In a bowl, mix flour, baking powder, and salt.
3. In another bowl, beat together sugar, cream cheese, eggs, and vanilla until smooth.
4. Gradually mix in the dry ingredients until just combined.
5. Gently fold in blueberries.
6. Divide batter evenly among cupcake liners and bake for 18-20 minutes.
7. Cool and top with more blueberries and a cream cheese frosting.

Churro Cupcakes

Ingredients:

- 1 ½ cups all-purpose flour
- 1 tbsp sugar
- 1 tsp baking powder
- 1 tsp cinnamon
- ½ tsp salt
- 1 cup milk
- 2 eggs
- ½ cup vegetable oil
- 1 tsp vanilla extract
- Cinnamon sugar for coating

Instructions:

1. Preheat oven to 350°F (175°C) and line a muffin tin with paper liners.
2. In a bowl, mix flour, sugar, baking powder, cinnamon, and salt.
3. In another bowl, whisk together milk, eggs, oil, and vanilla.
4. Gradually combine the wet and dry ingredients until smooth.
5. Divide batter evenly among cupcake liners and bake for 18-20 minutes.
6. Cool and roll in cinnamon sugar.

Lemon Poppy Seed Cupcakes

Ingredients:

- 1 ½ cups all-purpose flour
- 1 tbsp sugar
- 1 tsp baking powder
- 1 tbsp poppy seeds
- ½ tsp salt
- 1 cup buttermilk
- 2 eggs
- ½ cup vegetable oil
- 1 tsp vanilla extract
- Zest of 1 lemon

Instructions:

1. Preheat oven to 350°F (175°C) and line a muffin tin with paper liners.
2. In a bowl, mix flour, sugar, baking powder, poppy seeds, and salt.
3. In another bowl, whisk together buttermilk, eggs, oil, vanilla, and lemon zest.
4. Gradually combine the wet and dry ingredients until smooth.
5. Divide batter evenly among cupcake liners and bake for 18-20 minutes.
6. Cool and frost with lemon buttercream.

Nutella-Filled Cupcakes

Ingredients:

- 1 ½ cups all-purpose flour
- 1 tbsp sugar
- 1 tsp baking powder
- ¼ tsp salt
- 1 cup milk
- 2 eggs
- ½ cup Nutella
- ½ cup vegetable oil
- 1 tsp vanilla extract

Instructions:

1. Preheat oven to 350°F (175°C) and line a muffin tin with paper liners.
2. In a bowl, mix flour, sugar, baking powder, and salt.
3. In another bowl, whisk together milk, eggs, oil, and vanilla.
4. Gradually combine the wet and dry ingredients until smooth.
5. Scoop half the batter into each cupcake liner, add a spoonful of Nutella, and cover with remaining batter.
6. Bake for 18-20 minutes.
7. Cool and frost with Nutella frosting.

Carrot Cake Cupcakes

Ingredients:

- 1 ½ cups all-purpose flour
- 1 tsp baking powder
- ½ tsp baking soda
- 1 tsp cinnamon
- ¼ tsp nutmeg
- 1 cup grated carrots
- 1 cup sugar
- 2 eggs
- ½ cup vegetable oil
- 1 tsp vanilla extract
- ½ cup chopped walnuts (optional)

Instructions:

1. Preheat oven to 350°F (175°C) and line a muffin tin with paper liners.
2. In a bowl, mix flour, baking powder, baking soda, cinnamon, and nutmeg.
3. In another bowl, whisk together sugar, eggs, oil, and vanilla.
4. Gradually combine the wet and dry ingredients until smooth.
5. Stir in grated carrots and walnuts.
6. Divide batter evenly among cupcake liners and bake for 18-20 minutes.
7. Cool and frost with cream cheese frosting.

Chocolate Mint Cupcakes

Ingredients:

- 1 ½ cups all-purpose flour
- 1 cup granulated sugar
- 1 tsp baking powder
- ½ cup unsweetened cocoa powder
- 1 egg
- ½ cup milk
- ½ cup vegetable oil
- 1 tsp vanilla extract
- ½ tsp peppermint extract
- ½ cup chocolate chips

Instructions:

1. Preheat oven to 350°F (175°C) and line a muffin tin with paper liners.
2. In a bowl, mix flour, sugar, baking powder, and cocoa powder.
3. In another bowl, whisk together egg, milk, oil, vanilla, and peppermint extract.
4. Gradually combine the wet and dry ingredients until smooth.
5. Fold in chocolate chips.
6. Bake for 18-20 minutes, then cool and frost with mint chocolate frosting.

Cherry Almond Cupcakes

Ingredients:

- 1 ½ cups all-purpose flour
- 1 tbsp sugar
- 1 tsp baking powder
- ½ tsp almond extract
- 1 cup buttermilk
- 2 eggs
- ¼ cup chopped cherries
- ¼ cup chopped almonds
- 2 tbsp melted butter

Instructions:

1. Preheat oven to 350°F (175°C) and line a muffin tin with paper liners.
2. In a bowl, mix flour, sugar, and baking powder.
3. In another bowl, whisk together buttermilk, eggs, almond extract, and melted butter.
4. Stir the wet ingredients into the dry ingredients.
5. Fold in chopped cherries and almonds.
6. Bake for 18-20 minutes and cool.
7. Frost with almond-flavored buttercream and garnish with more chopped almonds.

Tiramisu Cupcakes

Ingredients:

- 1 ½ cups all-purpose flour
- 1 tsp baking powder
- ½ tsp baking soda
- ¼ tsp salt
- 1 cup granulated sugar
- 2 large eggs
- ½ cup sour cream
- ½ cup brewed espresso, cooled
- ½ tsp vanilla extract
- ¼ cup coffee liqueur (optional)
- ½ cup mascarpone cheese
- Cocoa powder for dusting

Instructions:

1. Preheat oven to 350°F (175°C) and line a muffin tin with paper liners.
2. In a bowl, mix flour, baking powder, baking soda, and salt.
3. In another bowl, whisk sugar and eggs until light and fluffy, then add sour cream, espresso, vanilla, and coffee liqueur.
4. Gradually add the dry ingredients and mix until smooth.
5. Spoon the batter into cupcake liners and bake for 18-20 minutes.
6. Cool the cupcakes and top with a dollop of mascarpone cheese.
7. Dust with cocoa powder before serving.

Lavender Honey Cupcakes

Ingredients:

- 1 ½ cups all-purpose flour
- 1 tbsp lavender buds, dried
- 1 tsp baking powder
- ½ tsp baking soda
- ½ tsp salt
- ½ cup unsalted butter, softened
- ¾ cup granulated sugar
- 2 large eggs
- 1 tsp vanilla extract
- ½ cup honey
- ½ cup buttermilk

Instructions:

1. Preheat oven to 350°F (175°C) and line a muffin tin with paper liners.
2. In a bowl, mix flour, lavender buds, baking powder, baking soda, and salt.
3. In another bowl, cream butter and sugar until fluffy. Add eggs one at a time, followed by vanilla and honey.
4. Gradually mix in dry ingredients, alternating with buttermilk.
5. Fill the cupcake liners with batter and bake for 18-20 minutes.
6. Cool and drizzle with honey or lavender buttercream.

Key Lime Pie Cupcakes

Ingredients:

- 1 ½ cups all-purpose flour
- 1 tsp baking powder
- ½ tsp baking soda
- ¼ tsp salt
- ½ cup unsalted butter, softened
- 1 cup granulated sugar
- 2 large eggs
- 1 tsp vanilla extract
- 1/2 cup key lime juice
- ½ cup buttermilk
- ½ cup graham cracker crumbs

Instructions:

1. Preheat oven to 350°F (175°C) and line a muffin tin with paper liners.
2. In a bowl, mix flour, baking powder, baking soda, and salt.
3. In another bowl, cream butter and sugar until fluffy. Add eggs and vanilla, then mix in lime juice and buttermilk.
4. Gradually stir in dry ingredients until smooth.
5. Fold in graham cracker crumbs.
6. Fill cupcake liners with batter and bake for 18-20 minutes.
7. Cool and frost with key lime pie buttercream or whipped cream.

Chocolate Hazelnut Cupcakes

Ingredients:

- 1 ½ cups all-purpose flour
- 1 cup granulated sugar
- 1 tsp baking powder
- ½ tsp baking soda
- ¼ tsp salt
- ½ cup unsweetened cocoa powder
- 2 large eggs
- ½ cup milk
- ½ cup vegetable oil
- 1 tsp vanilla extract
- ½ cup hazelnut spread (like Nutella)

Instructions:

1. Preheat oven to 350°F (175°C) and line a muffin tin with paper liners.
2. In a bowl, mix flour, sugar, baking powder, baking soda, salt, and cocoa powder.
3. In another bowl, whisk eggs, milk, oil, and vanilla.
4. Gradually combine wet and dry ingredients until smooth.
5. Spoon batter into cupcake liners, adding a spoonful of hazelnut spread in the center of each.
6. Bake for 18-20 minutes and cool.
7. Frost with hazelnut buttercream and drizzle with more hazelnut spread.

Coconut Pineapple Cupcakes

Ingredients:

- 1 ½ cups all-purpose flour
- 1 tsp baking powder
- ½ tsp baking soda
- ¼ tsp salt
- ½ cup unsalted butter, softened
- ¾ cup granulated sugar
- 2 large eggs
- ½ cup coconut milk
- ½ cup crushed pineapple, drained
- ½ cup shredded coconut

Instructions:

1. Preheat oven to 350°F (175°C) and line a muffin tin with paper liners.
2. In a bowl, mix flour, baking powder, baking soda, and salt.
3. In another bowl, cream butter and sugar until light and fluffy. Add eggs, coconut milk, pineapple, and shredded coconut.
4. Gradually add dry ingredients and mix until smooth.
5. Fill cupcake liners with batter and bake for 18-20 minutes.
6. Cool and frost with coconut buttercream.

Champagne Cupcakes

Ingredients:

- 1 ½ cups all-purpose flour
- 1 ½ tsp baking powder
- ¼ tsp salt
- ½ cup unsalted butter, softened
- 1 cup granulated sugar
- 2 large eggs
- 1 tsp vanilla extract
- ½ cup champagne or sparkling wine
- 1 tbsp lemon juice

Instructions:

1. Preheat oven to 350°F (175°C) and line a muffin tin with paper liners.
2. In a bowl, mix flour, baking powder, and salt.
3. In another bowl, cream butter and sugar until light and fluffy. Add eggs and vanilla, then mix in champagne and lemon juice.
4. Gradually stir in dry ingredients until smooth.
5. Fill cupcake liners with batter and bake for 18-20 minutes.
6. Cool and top with champagne buttercream or whipped cream.

Cookies and Cream Cupcakes

Ingredients:

- 1 ½ cups all-purpose flour
- 1 tsp baking powder
- 1 tsp baking soda
- ½ tsp salt
- ½ cup unsalted butter, softened
- 1 cup granulated sugar
- 2 large eggs
- 1 tsp vanilla extract
- 1 cup milk
- 10 Oreo cookies, crushed

Instructions:

1. Preheat oven to 350°F (175°C) and line a muffin tin with paper liners.
2. In a bowl, mix flour, baking powder, baking soda, and salt.
3. In another bowl, cream butter and sugar until fluffy. Add eggs and vanilla, then mix in milk.
4. Gradually stir in dry ingredients until smooth.
5. Gently fold in crushed Oreo cookies.
6. Bake for 18-20 minutes, then cool.
7. Frost with cookies and cream frosting and garnish with more Oreo crumbs.

Pineapple Upside-Down Cupcakes

Ingredients:

- 1 ½ cups all-purpose flour
- 1 tsp baking powder
- ½ tsp baking soda
- ¼ tsp salt
- ½ cup unsalted butter, softened
- ¾ cup brown sugar
- 2 large eggs
- ½ cup pineapple juice
- ½ cup milk
- 6-8 pineapple rings, cut into small pieces
- Maraschino cherries

Instructions:

1. Preheat oven to 350°F (175°C) and line a muffin tin with paper liners.
2. In a bowl, mix flour, baking powder, baking soda, and salt.
3. In another bowl, cream butter and brown sugar until fluffy. Add eggs and mix well.
4. Stir in pineapple juice and milk, then gradually add dry ingredients until smooth.
5. Spoon small amounts of batter into each cupcake liner and top with pineapple pieces and a cherry.
6. Bake for 18-20 minutes, then cool and invert the cupcakes.

White Chocolate Raspberry Cupcakes

Ingredients:

- 1 ½ cups all-purpose flour
- 1 tsp baking powder
- ¼ tsp salt
- ½ cup unsalted butter, softened
- 1 cup granulated sugar
- 2 large eggs
- 1 tsp vanilla extract
- ½ cup milk
- ½ cup white chocolate chips
- ½ cup fresh raspberries

Instructions:

1. Preheat oven to 350°F (175°C) and line a muffin tin with paper liners.
2. In a bowl, mix flour, baking powder, and salt.
3. In another bowl, cream butter and sugar until light and fluffy. Add eggs and vanilla, then mix in milk.
4. Gradually stir in dry ingredients and fold in white chocolate chips and raspberries.
5. Divide batter evenly and bake for 18-20 minutes.
6. Cool and frost with white chocolate raspberry buttercream.

Maple Bacon Cupcakes

Ingredients:

- 1 ½ cups all-purpose flour
- 1 tsp baking powder
- ½ tsp baking soda
- ¼ tsp salt
- ½ cup unsalted butter, softened
- ¾ cup granulated sugar
- 2 large eggs
- 1 tsp vanilla extract
- ½ cup buttermilk
- ½ cup maple syrup
- ¼ cup cooked bacon, chopped

Instructions:

1. Preheat oven to 350°F (175°C) and line a muffin tin with paper liners.
2. In a bowl, mix flour, baking powder, baking soda, and salt.
3. In another bowl, cream butter and sugar until fluffy. Add eggs and vanilla, then mix in buttermilk and maple syrup.
4. Gradually stir in dry ingredients and fold in chopped bacon.
5. Bake for 18-20 minutes and cool.
6. Frost with maple buttercream and top with crispy bacon.

Cinnamon Roll Cupcakes

Ingredients:

- 1 ½ cups all-purpose flour
- 1 tsp baking powder
- 1 tsp cinnamon
- ½ cup unsalted butter, softened
- 1 cup granulated sugar
- 2 large eggs
- 1 tsp vanilla extract
- ½ cup milk
- Cinnamon sugar for filling

Instructions:

1. Preheat oven to 350°F (175°C) and line a muffin tin with paper liners.
2. In a bowl, mix flour, baking powder, and cinnamon.
3. In another bowl, cream butter and sugar until fluffy, then add eggs and vanilla.
4. Gradually add the dry ingredients and milk until smooth.
5. Spoon half the batter into cupcake liners, sprinkle with cinnamon sugar, then top with the remaining batter.
6. Bake for 18-20 minutes and frost with cinnamon glaze.

Hot Cocoa Cupcakes

Ingredients:

- 1 ½ cups all-purpose flour
- 1 cup granulated sugar
- ½ cup unsweetened cocoa powder
- 1 tsp baking powder
- ½ tsp baking soda
- ¼ tsp salt
- 2 large eggs
- 1 cup milk
- ½ cup vegetable oil
- 1 tsp vanilla extract
- ½ cup hot cocoa mix

Instructions:

1. Preheat oven to 350°F (175°C) and line a muffin tin with paper liners.
2. In a bowl, whisk flour, sugar, cocoa powder, baking powder, baking soda, salt, and hot cocoa mix.
3. In another bowl, whisk eggs, milk, oil, and vanilla.
4. Gradually combine wet and dry ingredients, mixing until smooth.
5. Divide the batter evenly and bake for 18-20 minutes.
6. Cool and frost with hot cocoa-flavored buttercream.

White Chocolate Macadamia Cupcakes

Ingredients:

- 1 ½ cups all-purpose flour
- 1 tsp baking powder
- ½ tsp salt
- ½ cup unsalted butter, softened
- 1 cup granulated sugar
- 2 large eggs
- 1 tsp vanilla extract
- ½ cup milk
- ½ cup white chocolate chips
- ½ cup chopped macadamia nuts

Instructions:

1. Preheat oven to 350°F (175°C) and line a muffin tin with paper liners.
2. In a bowl, mix flour, baking powder, and salt.
3. In another bowl, cream butter and sugar until fluffy. Add eggs and vanilla.
4. Gradually stir in dry ingredients and milk until smooth.
5. Fold in white chocolate chips and macadamia nuts.
6. Bake for 18-20 minutes, then cool.
7. Frost with white chocolate buttercream.

Mocha Hazelnut Cupcakes

Ingredients:

- 1 ½ cups all-purpose flour
- 1 cup granulated sugar
- 1 tsp baking powder
- 1 tsp instant coffee granules
- ¼ tsp salt
- 2 large eggs
- ½ cup milk
- ½ cup vegetable oil
- 1 tsp vanilla extract
- ½ cup hazelnut spread

Instructions:

1. Preheat oven to 350°F (175°C) and line a muffin tin with paper liners.
2. In a bowl, mix flour, sugar, baking powder, coffee granules, and salt.
3. In another bowl, whisk eggs, milk, oil, and vanilla.
4. Combine wet and dry ingredients until smooth.
5. Fold in hazelnut spread.
6. Bake for 18-20 minutes.
7. Cool and frost with mocha buttercream or whipped cream.

Mint Chocolate Chip Cupcakes

Ingredients:

- 1 ½ cups all-purpose flour
- 1 tsp baking powder
- ½ tsp salt
- ½ cup unsalted butter, softened
- 1 cup granulated sugar
- 2 large eggs
- 1 tsp vanilla extract
- ½ tsp mint extract
- ½ cup milk
- ½ cup mini chocolate chips

Instructions:

1. Preheat oven to 350°F (175°C) and line a muffin tin with paper liners.
2. In a bowl, mix flour, baking powder, and salt.
3. In another bowl, cream butter and sugar until fluffy, then add eggs, vanilla, and mint extract.
4. Gradually add the dry ingredients and milk until smooth.
5. Fold in chocolate chips.
6. Bake for 18-20 minutes, then cool.
7. Frost with mint buttercream and more chocolate chips.

Peanut Butter Banana Cupcakes

Ingredients:

- 1 ½ cups all-purpose flour
- 1 tsp baking powder
- ½ tsp baking soda
- ¼ tsp salt
- ½ cup unsalted butter, softened
- 1 cup granulated sugar
- 2 large eggs
- 1 ripe banana, mashed
- ½ cup peanut butter
- ½ cup milk

Instructions:

1. Preheat oven to 350°F (175°C) and line a muffin tin with paper liners.
2. In a bowl, mix flour, baking powder, baking soda, and salt.
3. In another bowl, cream butter and sugar until fluffy, then add eggs, banana, and peanut butter.
4. Gradually add the dry ingredients and milk, mixing until smooth.
5. Bake for 18-20 minutes, then cool.
6. Frost with peanut butter frosting or chocolate ganache.

Oreo Cupcakes

Ingredients:

- 1 ½ cups all-purpose flour
- 1 tsp baking powder
- ½ tsp baking soda
- ¼ tsp salt
- 1 cup granulated sugar
- 2 large eggs
- ½ cup unsalted butter, softened
- 1 cup milk
- 6 Oreo cookies, crushed

Instructions:

1. Preheat oven to 350°F (175°C) and line a muffin tin with paper liners.
2. In a bowl, mix flour, baking powder, baking soda, and salt.
3. In another bowl, cream butter and sugar until fluffy, then add eggs and milk.
4. Gradually stir in dry ingredients until smooth.
5. Fold in crushed Oreos.
6. Bake for 18-20 minutes, then cool.
7. Frost with cookies and cream frosting and garnish with an Oreo cookie.

Apple Cinnamon Cupcakes

Ingredients:

- 1 ½ cups all-purpose flour
- 1 tsp baking powder
- 1 tsp cinnamon
- ¼ tsp nutmeg
- ½ tsp salt
- 1 cup granulated sugar
- 2 large eggs
- 1 cup unsweetened applesauce
- ½ cup vegetable oil
- 1 tsp vanilla extract

Instructions:

1. Preheat oven to 350°F (175°C) and line a muffin tin with paper liners.
2. In a bowl, mix flour, baking powder, cinnamon, nutmeg, and salt.
3. In another bowl, whisk sugar, eggs, applesauce, oil, and vanilla.
4. Gradually stir in the dry ingredients until smooth.
5. Divide the batter evenly among the cupcake liners and bake for 18-20 minutes.
6. Cool and frost with cinnamon buttercream.

Chocolate Cherry Cupcakes

Ingredients:

- 1 ½ cups all-purpose flour
- 1 cup granulated sugar
- ½ cup unsweetened cocoa powder
- 1 tsp baking powder
- ½ tsp baking soda
- ¼ tsp salt
- 2 large eggs
- 1 cup milk
- ½ cup vegetable oil
- ½ cup maraschino cherries, chopped

Instructions:

1. Preheat oven to 350°F (175°C) and line a muffin tin with paper liners.
2. In a bowl, mix flour, sugar, cocoa powder, baking powder, baking soda, and salt.
3. In another bowl, whisk eggs, milk, and oil.
4. Gradually stir the wet ingredients into the dry ingredients until smooth.
5. Gently fold in chopped cherries.
6. Bake for 18-20 minutes, then cool.
7. Frost with chocolate or cherry frosting.

Pecan Praline Cupcakes

Ingredients:

- 1 ½ cups all-purpose flour
- 1 tsp baking powder
- ½ tsp baking soda
- ¼ tsp salt
- 1 cup granulated sugar
- ½ cup unsalted butter, softened
- 2 large eggs
- ½ cup buttermilk
- ½ cup chopped pecans

Instructions:

1. Preheat oven to 350°F (175°C) and line a muffin tin with paper liners.
2. In a bowl, mix flour, baking powder, baking soda, and salt.
3. In another bowl, cream butter and sugar until fluffy. Add eggs, one at a time, then mix in buttermilk.
4. Gradually add the dry ingredients until smooth.
5. Fold in chopped pecans.
6. Bake for 18-20 minutes, then cool.
7. Frost with praline buttercream and top with more pecans.

Funfetti Birthday Cupcakes

Ingredients:

- 1 ½ cups all-purpose flour
- 1 tsp baking powder
- ½ tsp salt
- 1 cup granulated sugar
- ½ cup unsalted butter, softened
- 2 large eggs
- 1 tsp vanilla extract
- ½ cup buttermilk
- ½ cup sprinkles

Instructions:

1. Preheat oven to 350°F (175°C) and line a muffin tin with paper liners.
2. In a bowl, mix flour, baking powder, and salt.
3. In another bowl, cream butter and sugar until fluffy. Add eggs and vanilla.
4. Gradually stir in dry ingredients and buttermilk.
5. Fold in sprinkles.
6. Divide batter into cupcake liners and bake for 18-20 minutes.
7. Frost with birthday cake buttercream and top with more sprinkles.

Chocolate Raspberry Ganache Cupcakes

Ingredients:

- 1 ½ cups all-purpose flour
- 1 cup granulated sugar
- ½ cup unsweetened cocoa powder
- 1 tsp baking powder
- ½ tsp baking soda
- ¼ tsp salt
- 2 large eggs
- ½ cup milk
- ½ cup vegetable oil
- 1 tsp vanilla extract
- ½ cup fresh raspberries

Instructions:

1. Preheat oven to 350°F (175°C) and line a muffin tin with paper liners.
2. In a bowl, mix flour, sugar, cocoa powder, baking powder, baking soda, and salt.
3. In another bowl, whisk eggs, milk, oil, and vanilla.
4. Gradually combine wet and dry ingredients until smooth.
5. Gently fold in raspberries.
6. Bake for 18-20 minutes, then cool.
7. Top with chocolate ganache and raspberries.

Blackberry Lemon Cupcakes

Ingredients:

- 1 ½ cups all-purpose flour
- 1 tsp baking powder
- ½ tsp baking soda
- ¼ tsp salt
- 1 cup granulated sugar
- ½ cup unsalted butter, softened
- 2 large eggs
- 1 tsp vanilla extract
- 1 tsp lemon zest
- ½ cup milk
- ½ cup fresh blackberries, mashed

Instructions:

1. Preheat oven to 350°F (175°C) and line a muffin tin with paper liners.
2. In a bowl, mix flour, baking powder, baking soda, and salt.
3. In another bowl, cream butter and sugar until light and fluffy. Add eggs, vanilla, and lemon zest.
4. Gradually add the dry ingredients and milk, mixing until smooth.
5. Gently fold in mashed blackberries.
6. Divide the batter evenly and bake for 18-20 minutes.
7. Cool and frost with lemon buttercream and fresh blackberries.

Red Wine Chocolate Cupcakes

Ingredients:

- 1 ½ cups all-purpose flour
- ¾ cup unsweetened cocoa powder
- 1 tsp baking powder
- 1 tsp baking soda
- ¼ tsp salt
- 1 cup granulated sugar
- ½ cup unsalted butter, softened
- 2 large eggs
- 1 tsp vanilla extract
- ¾ cup red wine (such as Cabernet or Merlot)
- ½ cup milk

Instructions:

1. Preheat oven to 350°F (175°C) and line a muffin tin with paper liners.
2. In a bowl, mix flour, cocoa powder, baking powder, baking soda, and salt.
3. In another bowl, cream butter and sugar until light and fluffy. Add eggs and vanilla.
4. Gradually add the dry ingredients, alternating with the red wine and milk, mixing until smooth.
5. Divide the batter evenly and bake for 18-20 minutes.
6. Cool and frost with chocolate ganache or red wine buttercream.

Butter Pecan Cupcakes

Ingredients:

- 1 ½ cups all-purpose flour
- 1 tsp baking powder
- ¼ tsp salt
- ½ cup unsalted butter, softened
- 1 cup granulated sugar
- 2 large eggs
- 1 tsp vanilla extract
- ½ cup milk
- ½ cup toasted pecans, chopped

Instructions:

1. Preheat oven to 350°F (175°C) and line a muffin tin with paper liners.
2. In a bowl, mix flour, baking powder, and salt.
3. In another bowl, cream butter and sugar until fluffy. Add eggs and vanilla.
4. Gradually stir in the dry ingredients and milk until smooth.
5. Fold in toasted pecans.
6. Bake for 18-20 minutes, then cool.
7. Frost with butter pecan buttercream and sprinkle with more chopped pecans.

Dark Chocolate Espresso Cupcakes

Ingredients:

- 1 ½ cups all-purpose flour
- 1 cup granulated sugar
- ½ cup unsweetened cocoa powder
- 1 tsp baking powder
- ½ tsp baking soda
- ¼ tsp salt
- 2 large eggs
- 1 tsp vanilla extract
- ½ cup brewed espresso, cooled
- ½ cup milk

Instructions:

1. Preheat oven to 350°F (175°C) and line a muffin tin with paper liners.
2. In a bowl, mix flour, sugar, cocoa powder, baking powder, baking soda, and salt.
3. In another bowl, whisk eggs, vanilla, espresso, and milk.
4. Gradually combine wet and dry ingredients until smooth.
5. Divide the batter evenly and bake for 18-20 minutes.
6. Cool and frost with espresso buttercream or dark chocolate ganache.

Maple Pecan Cupcakes

Ingredients:

- 1 ½ cups all-purpose flour
- 1 tsp baking powder
- ½ tsp baking soda
- ¼ tsp salt
- ½ cup unsalted butter, softened
- 1 cup granulated sugar
- 2 large eggs
- 1 tsp vanilla extract
- ½ cup buttermilk
- ½ cup maple syrup
- ½ cup chopped pecans

Instructions:

1. Preheat oven to 350°F (175°C) and line a muffin tin with paper liners.
2. In a bowl, mix flour, baking powder, baking soda, and salt.
3. In another bowl, cream butter and sugar until fluffy. Add eggs, vanilla, and maple syrup.
4. Gradually add dry ingredients and buttermilk, mixing until smooth.
5. Fold in chopped pecans.
6. Divide the batter evenly and bake for 18-20 minutes.
7. Cool and frost with maple buttercream and sprinkle with more pecans.

Gingerbread Cupcakes

Ingredients:

- 1 ½ cups all-purpose flour
- 1 tsp baking powder
- 1 tsp ground ginger
- 1 tsp ground cinnamon
- ¼ tsp ground cloves
- ¼ tsp salt
- 1 cup granulated sugar
- ½ cup unsalted butter, softened
- 2 large eggs
- ½ cup molasses
- ½ cup buttermilk

Instructions:

1. Preheat oven to 350°F (175°C) and line a muffin tin with paper liners.
2. In a bowl, mix flour, baking powder, ginger, cinnamon, cloves, and salt.
3. In another bowl, cream butter and sugar until light and fluffy. Add eggs and molasses.
4. Gradually add dry ingredients and buttermilk, mixing until smooth.
5. Divide the batter evenly and bake for 18-20 minutes.
6. Cool and frost with cinnamon cream cheese frosting.

www.ingramcontent.com/pod-product-compliance
Lightning Source LLC
LaVergne TN
LVHW081336060526
838201LV00055B/2680